Tadpole Books are published by Jump!, 5357 Penn Avenue South, Minneapolis, MN 55419, www.jumplibrary.com

Copyright ©2023 Jump. International copyright reserved in all countries. No part of this book may be reproduced in any form without written permission from the publisher.

Editor: Jenna Gleisner **Designer:** Molly Ballanger **Translator:** Annette Granat

Photo Credits: MidoSemsem/Shutterstock, cover; adutt/Shutterstock, 1; BJI/Blue Jean Images/Getty, 2ml, 3; Anna Krivitskaya/Shutterstock, 2tl, 4–5; Goodboy Picture Company/iStock, 2mr, 6–7; Hakase_/iStock, 2tr, 8–9; SolStock/iStock, 2bl, 10–11; Nanette Dreyer/Shutterstock, 2br, 12–13; Africa Studio/Shutterstock, 14–15; Spotmatik/iStock, 16tl; Dishant Shrivastava/Shutterstock, 16tr; Boogich/iStock, 16bl; kali9/iStock, 16br.

Library of Congress Cataloging-in-Publication Data
Names: Gleisner, Jenna Lee, author.
Title: Los ejercicios físicos / por Jenna Lee Gleisner.
Other titles: Exercising. Spanish
Description: Minneapolis, MN: Jump!, Inc., 2023.
Series: Las primeras rutinas | Includes index. | Audience: Ages 4–7
Identifiers: LCCN 2021059754 (print)
LCCN 2021059755 (ebook)
ISBN 9798885240260 (hardcover)
ISBN 9798885240277 (paperback)
ISBN 9798885240284 (ebook)
Subjects: LCSH: Exercise—Juvenile literature. | Exercise for children—Juvenile literature.
Physical fitness for children—Juvenile literature.
Classification: LCC GV481 .G5518 2023 (print) | LCC GV481 (ebook) | DDC 613.7/1083—dc23/eng/20211222
LC record available at https://lccn.loc.gov/2021059754
LC ebook record available at https://lccn.loc.gov/2021059755

LAS PRIMERAS RUTINAS
LOS EJERCICIOS FÍSICOS

por Jenna Lee Gleisner

TABLA DE CONTENIDO

Palabras a saber	2
Los ejercicios físicos	3
¡Repasemos!	16
Índice	16

PALABRAS A SABER

bailo

brinco

camino

corro

juego

salto

LOS EJERCICIOS FÍSICOS

Yo camino.

Yo corro.

Yo brinco.

Yo salto.

¡REPASEMOS!

¡Hay muchas maneras de mover el cuerpo! ¿Cuáles ejercicios físicos están haciendo estas personas?

ÍNDICE

bailo 5
brinco 9
camino 3
corro 7

juego 11
salto 13, 15
salto a la cuerda 15